Matilda & Maxwell™

FREAKY!!
HOMEWORK
FIASCO

by Dr. Stephanie Donaldson-Pressman

Dr. Robert Pressman

illustrated by Lisa Petty

Matilda & Maxwell's Homework Fiasco!
Copyright © 2025 by Good Parent, Inc. Publishers.
Printed in the United States of America.

A GoodParentGoodChild® Book
ISBN-13 9780983218333

Book design and composition: Anette Schuetz

Publication Consultant: www.formatting.com

We have some very cool friends, who helped us a lot with *organizing* (that word should be on the Naughty Word List!) this totally awesome book. BFF's Ella Bennison and Gigi Mattson let us borrow their stupendous (amazing, terrific) sayings: *NWL* and *Happy Exclamation Points!!* XO ☺

Mostly, Bobby Jackson (13) Emma Lou Jacque (12) and Marie Balemian (9) — three amazing friends who read our Journals (the parts we gave them, anyway) and told us what was "too lame" or "cool." Thanks, you guys.

And there was one grown-up who does all kinds of art things on the computer, Anette Schuetz. She helped us make our book look really good. Wonder if she'd help kids with Science Fair projects?

Matilda & Maxwell™

CHAPTER ONE:

The 1st Day OF School

Pul-eeze!

Matilda's Journal

Matilda

—MEMO—

From the desk of Augustus P. Reilly, Ed.D.
Chichester County Superintendent of Schools

Dear Students and Parents:

Welcome back to school! We hope that your summer was full of fun! This year, thanks to our new Coordinator of Student Affairs, Mrs. Colleen Shapely, each student at the Chichester Middle School (grades 5–8) will be keeping a Homework Journal. Mrs. Shapely, who recently received her Ph.D. in Counseling and Student Services (kudos to you, Mrs. Shapely), has received a USA grant. She will test the value of student homework journals in the education retention process. These journals will not be read, per se, by the teachers. They will be checked from time to time to ensure that daily entries are being made. All students are being issued a journal. Make certain that your student has brought his/hers home with him/her.

What a tool! "Augustus." Who names their kid "Augustus"? My dad calls him "A–GAS–tush" because he talks all the time at School Bored meetings (my dad says they are so–o–o boring) and the room always smells like farts. Ma Mere (she hates that I call her that because it sounds like she's a horse) hates that he talks about **farts** in front of me. I usually say something like,

"Father, do you mean an explosion of gaseous fumes from the rectum?" Mom hates the word **rectum** even more than **fart.** As you can tell,

Eee-uw!!

we have *scintillating* (sparkling, dazzling, brilliant) dinner table conversations in my house. LOL.

Sometimes I wish I had an older brother or sister, like Maxwell does. His older brother, Austin, is so cool — really, he's so cute! Of course, if he were my older brother, he wouldn't be cute — or I couldn't think he was cute — whatever. That's a disgusting thought.

SO CUTE.

Anywho — this is Alyssa's new fav saying — it's kind of lame, but I can't seem to stop using it. I REALLY think it's a dumb word — why can't I stop it from coming into my brain??? (Alyssa has now moved up to being my #3 best friend in the world, after Astrid and, of course, Maxwell.)

What was I talking about? Oh! Anyway — we got a notice about this sincerely dumb

Journal thing. In the first place, there are so many things that are just **so wrong** about the totally random notice, that I don't even know where to start.

soo... lame!

OK. "From the desk of…" Like, the desk knows how to write? The desk is actually the one in charge, the big boss? "Wait, I need to consult my desk!" or, "Let's see what the desk thinks." I mean, Pul-eeze! Uncool. Bad — and not in the good way.

Then, of course, we have the kissing up to Mrs. Shapely, whoever she is. Followed by the astonishing news for total idiots who have severe short-term memory problems that Chichester Middle School is — gulp! — grades 5–8. OMG! Really? When did that happen?

Next we have "kudos." I had to look that one up: "Praise, credit, or glory for an achievement." Sounds more like "coo-doz": a gross, nasty, "crème"-filled pastry for short, fat, mustached old ladies with a shelf life of 2000 years. The pastry has a shelf life, not the ladies. I can see the commercial now:

"Coo-doz…when 10 Twinkies just aren't enough!"

But the best is – "the education retention process." Education retention. It sounds like a disease: "Just a little shot

with this big, fat needle, and we'll take care of that painful 'education retention' problem!!" I think that **education retention**

MUST go on my Naughty Word List (NWL). Hmm. **Rectum,** too. Yuck!

Well, we'll see if they really do **not** read our Journals…per se or no per se. Sounds Spanish: "Do you know where the nearest

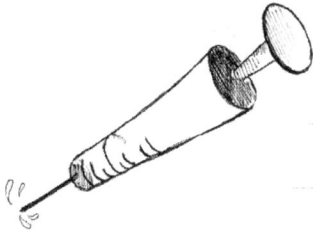

hospital is?" "No per se, Señor!"

$20 says they'll try to trick us like they always do. Like, not checking it for 3 weeks, and then one day they say, "Journals out!" And they go down the rows and mark everybody off. They don't mark the people, just the Journals...if they have them and if they are written in. So you need to have...essentially... per se...180 Journal entries, give or take. Well, mark me down for Numero Uno, Señor.

Gotta go and call Astrid — that was hilarious about Maxwell!!!

Ciao,

Matilda ♥

CHAPTER TWO:

Why Should THIS Year Be Different?

Maxwell's Journal

Maxwell

This is so stupid. The first day of school. Stupid. I just sat there, looking out the window, sweating my butt off. No AC. Must have been 100° in that smelly room. Franklin, one of my best friends (except for Matilda, but she doesn't count — it's not that she doesn't count — she'd be peed off if she read that — which she never will — but you don't really talk about your best friend being a girl), said, "We just need to try a little mind control, and then this won't seem so bad." Okay. That sounds good. "Just imagine that you're not really here." Good, so far. "You're on a vacation at the beach." Great! "You're actually a lobster, and you're now in a big, smelly pot of boiling water!"

Yeah, really great Franklin. Thanks a lot!

Matilda is actually pretty cool. And she's wickedly funny. I mean, wicked EVIL. But I really, honestly wanted to vaporize her today. Can someone please tell me, why is it that girls are ALWAYS the ones that think up the really bad stuff, but it's ALWAYS boys who get caught doing it?

Today is the perfect example. First day of school, itchy clothes that my Mom made me wear. I don't know what it is about the first day of school. Why do you have to wear stupid clothes that itch and look dumb, when the next day you're going in shorts and a T-shirt?

Stupid. It's like that "this is the first day of the rest of your life" junk. I hope not.

Here's what happened. I have Mrs. Ward for homeroom AND social studies, excuse me, American History 1. We are sitting down, and I say something to Matilda about Mrs. Ward, and she says, "Mrs. Ward? Did you call her Mrs. Ward? Her name is Mrs. WART!" And she says it real serious.

I say, "Are you sure?" And she says, "Look. She has this big, honkin' wart on her nose, and she took some kind of empowerment class or something, and they told her to embrace her flaws. So, she decided to take the bull by the horns and face her flaw head on. Hence (she always uses words like hence... she reads books for *fun*) "the name change, to **Wart.** See? She wrote it up there, on the board. Didn't she, Astrid?"

Astrid says, "Oh, yeah. Totally. My Aunt Kristine was in the same class."

Well, I looked, and sure enough, there it was: "Mrs. Wart."

So Mrs. Wart comes in, and she wants us to sit in alphabetical order, so she

can "get to know us better." Right. It's so she knows where to look when she hears fart sounds!

She starts to sit, and she says, "Is there a Maxwell in here? Maxwell Pierce?" and I think, "Seriously? School hasn't even started yet and I'm in trouble already!"

She looks around, and Franklin says, pointing to me, "Ma'am" (he's such a kiss-up) "he's Maxwell Pierce."

And she goes, "Are you Austin's brother?"

I hear a nasty chuckle from
Franklin, who starts making
kissy sounds and whispering,
"Ooh! I just LOVE your big
brother Austin!"

And I'm really afraid
she's going to hear Franklin
and then I'll somehow be the one who gets
blamed, so I say, "Um, yes, Mrs. Wart. I'm
Maxwell."

And, suddenly, it's like those TV
commercials where the room gets instantly
quiet. She gets a funny look on her face,
and she goes, "What did you say?"

I said, "I'm Maxwell…Ma'am." (I figured if
it works for Franklin — which it always does
— then it might work for me. Wrong, again.)

"Young man" (you know you're in trouble
when they start calling you young man) "what
did you call me?" Now she has this weird
smile on her face. It's way scarier than the
funny look was.

I start to sweat. Great! Now I'll be in trouble AND smell like a llama! "Um, your name, Ma'am." I choke.

"What name?" she asks, real quiet. You know how they always say, "You could hear a pin drop?" Well, I swear, you could hear the beads of sweat dropping off my face onto the desk. Honest.

"Well, um, your name," I stammer, feeling like a total boogerhead.

"Your name…" I repeat, like a moron, and point at the board. She turns, and in that one micro-second I see it all. I have been played — set up — used. Somebody else wrote that on the board. Her name ISN'T REALLY MRS. WART!

In one smooth motion, she puts down her bag, and pulls out the yellow pad. As she starts to write, the warning buzzer sounds. I have my first detention, and school hasn't even officially started.

Welcome to the new school year. 179 days to go.

CHAPTER THREE:

Lunchroom Craziness!

Pul-eeze!

Matilda's Journal

Matilda

—MEMO—

From the desk of Francis J. German, Ed.D.
Principal, Chichester Middle School

Dear Students and Parents:

It has come to our attention that there have been several incidents of bad behavior in the lunchroom during second lunch. Popping of lunch bags, throwing of food, tampering with homework, borrowing of journals, and missing articles of clothing have been reported by Mrs. Lucille Wolfsteiger, Director of Cafetorium Services. If these behaviors do not stop immediately, our students will be required to lunch in their homerooms until Columbus Day. Thank you for your attention to this matter.

What a tool! Where do they find these fossils? Another old dude with a talking desk (Notorious Talking Desk — NTD)! If they actually tried to have a TV program about these gross old guys and their strange relationship with their desks, it would have to be on Old Fartito Cable. I don't even want to think about — to consider — the kinds of conversations they might have. Oh, what the...

NTD: "Good morning to you, Francis."

Francis: "And the top of the mornin' to you, too, old boy!" (OMG! They're even incredibly, scarily weird in my imagination!!!!!!! Somebody Help Me! SHM!)

NTD: "I say, those are some natty trousers you're wearing today, sir. Plaid! Very lame!"

No, no, and No! Now I am seriously freaking myself out. I won't even THINK about going there — the desks — the weird old guys. No. Uh-uh.

I gotta say, however, that these little missives (letter, memo, note) from our fearless leaders (like, "Take me to your leader because you are too old and strange to be from this planet!") provide me with hours of amusement.

When Ma Mere saw the latest, she said, "Matilda, you have second lunch this year, don't you?"

I earnestly (seriously, solemnly, gravely) replied, "Yes, Ma Mere, I do."

Mere: "You know I hate it when you call me that, Matilda. Have you noticed any of these…incidents?"

Hmmm. I wonder which "incident" in

particular she is referring to. Could it
be when Franklin yanked Jake's gym shorts
down so that Jake was displaying his white
butt to the entire backside (Ha! Ha!) of the
Cafetorium? (Perhaps I should call it the
Cafetori-rump as per Astrid.)

Or, maybe I could tell her about when Maxwell — seeing the display of white butt — spit out his mouthful of very bad lasagna, it was Lasagna Wednesday, and declaimed (made a speech, uttered, recited, or, in Max's case, uttered from the gutter), "Jacob! Glad to **see** you're *back*!"

Mrs. Lucy (as in "Lucifer, **a.k.a.** also known as, **Satan!**) got it all wrong, as usual, and sent poor Maxwell to the (Puke!) Principal's Office, home of the NTD (Notorious Talking Desk).

Or, maybe it's because Max, poor dolt (a rude word that insults somebody's intelligence — gosh, I just thought it meant *dummy!*), left his Journal on the table. Alyssa grabbed it and began to read it out loud. That was pretty hilarious! UNTIL she got to the part about how he got put next to Olivia (Wicked

Witch In Training — **WWIT**) in math. I yanked that sucker right out of her hands. After all, these are supposed to be

PRIVATE.

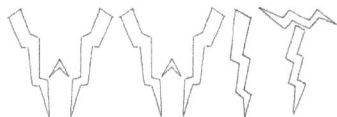

When I later perused (read in detail, examined, checked) his Journal, I could not help but notice that there is Nothing — Nada — Zero — Zilch after the first week of school — and that was only three days! Maxwell is going to be in DEEP poop if Mrs. ~~WART~~ Ward ever checks his Journal, which she hasn't since Day 3, **a.k.a.** the last day Maxwell journalled.

Anywho, yrs truly was so deeply distressed by Alyssa's reading (and mentioning Olivia the WWIT — puke!) that I had to:

1. Pop Alyssa's lunch bag, which had the unforeseen and most unfortunate effect of

2. mixing her pb&j with her grapes and

3. exploding her juice box. Oops!

4. Duck out of the way when Alyssa threw her sodden (saturated, soaked, wet) mess of a lunch at me — missing me, but

5. hitting Lucy, **a.k.a.** Lucifer the Devil(who had rolled over to see what was happening so she could report someone), directly in the hyper-mammary development area (boobs). Ooh! Most unfortunate.

6. I felt **really** bad when Lucy hauled Alyssa out of the Cafetorirump!!!!

cafetori-RUMP

Personally, I think she should file Assault charges against Mrs. Wolfsteiger, but as she is not speaking to me at this time, I can't give her the benefit of my advice.

Me to Mere: "No, mother. I think the

whole thing is the result of Mrs. Wolfsteiger's over-active imagination."

FYI: WWIT thinks she's **all that** with her long blond curls and her Juicy Gems Lip Gloss, and her satin training bras. Puke!

au revoir,

Matilda ♡

CHAPTER FOUR:

WHO Is In Charge of This Planet and WHY Do They Hate Me?!

Maxwell's Journal

Maxwell

My brother Austin (he who should be declared a God, according to my Mom and himself) was reading those stupid things in the paper about your birth sign — (astronomy?) at the breakfast table.

So, I'm trying to finish my math homework, my pencil breaks, we don't have a stupid pencil sharpener anywhere (Austin — of course — does his math in pen because he's so perfect), I get Cocoa Toasties with Raisins (which is actually pretty revolting but I have to eat them because I made my Mother buy them) all over my math paper, and when I try to wipe it up I rip the paper.

Austin sighs (like he's SERIOUSLY annoyed), takes out his pen, and finishes my math homework in the speed of light. Seriously — you can't even

see the pen move, and BAM! he's done. The guy is some kind of weird math genius. In addition to looking like that actor who plays the vampire — without the gold sparkly things and the pointy teeth — and being awesome in 3 varsity sports. Life, as my Grampa is always saying, is unfair. You think?

So Austin is reading about my sign — which is Cancer — how totally, awesomely perfect; my sign is a terminal disease — and it says, "Today is going to be full of challenges. Persevere, and you will triumph. Be aware of Virgo for the next three days, blah blah blah…" because his moons are up my butt or something like that.

So, knowing — before I even leave the house — that the day is going to be seriously bad news, since even the idiots who write the astronomy column know that "challenge" is adult-speak for hideous-problem-that-is-going-to-bite-your-butt, I was not expecting anything good to happen.

But, I was also not expecting the whole day to be a total, weird disaster of HUGE proportions. Today…I don't even know where to begin.

AARGH!!!

I AM NOT A BAD KID! SERIOUSLY!

Okay, now me, myself, and I know this. Unfortunately, the rest of the bonehead world has not tumbled to this fact.

The morning wasn't too bad. Once again,

Mrs. Ward did not ask for the Journals, which is good, because, along with most of my homework, I haven't written anything since… hmm. Since a long time.

I will say this now, for the record. I disagree with the whole principal (principle?) of homework. Not just because I hate it, which I do, but because it is SERIOUSLY RUINING MY LIFE! I like sports; I play most of them. I also like anything that is outside.

Here's what I like:

o Football

o Baseball

o Soccer

o Hockey

o Laser Tag

o Fishing

o Swimming

o Skiing

o Llama jokes on YouTube

o Pretty much ALL video games

Here's what I hate:

o Anything made with cabbage (it smells like PEE!)

🕷 HOMEWORK

Homework is for people who have no life. Like teachers, and those nerds who think running to the computer is a sport.

There are some people, like Matilda, who can do their homework and still do other stuff. She's not so into sports, except gymnastics, which is pretty hard, but she does all kinds of dance stuff, and I guess she's pretty good at it. And, she's still cool, in her strange Matilda-Queen-of-Drama way. But most of us are either regular guys or homework nerds.

I wouldn't even care so much if there was just LESS of it. Why do you need to have a kid do 50 math problems? Can't you tell from 5 if he knows it? Who really needs to do a Multi-Media Project on hibernation? They go to sleep when it's cold, their metabolism winds down; they get up when it's warm, their metabolism speeds up. What more, honestly, is there to say?

I really, sincerely hate homework. I do not see the need for it. I don't want to do it. It's hard, I never have all the stuff. That's what I want to say in this stupid Homework Journal — which is the stupidest homework assignment of all!

UGH.

It's not like I just got up one day and said, "No way am I going to do my homework! Not now, not ever." I really try, which is what's totally freaking me out. But, it's like, I was born under a black cloud — or something.

Take last night. I went to get my English
book, and it wasn't in my backpack. I swear
I put it in there. I went to my locker after
school especially to get it. Astrid came over
and we were talking about basketball tryouts
and stuff. Then Jake stopped by to invite me
over to his house to shoot some hoops, and
Olivia went by and *winked*
at me. At me! So, I go to
get the stupid book — not
there. Not in the house.
It's like the Miracle of
the Disappearing Book.
Which usually happens just
before the Miracle of the
Failing Grade.

Or, last week, the Miracle of the
Vanishing Backpack. Two times — not once,
but **TWICE last week** I walked all the way
home without noticing that I didn't have
my backpack. On Tuesday, I found it in the
locker room, which is really weird, because

I have Gym 6th period. Which means I had to go to Language Arts and real Art with no backpack. Then Friday, it turned up in the 2nd floor boys' bathroom. I don't even **remember** going there on Thursday!

Maybe someone is out to get me. They're taking my stuff and hiding it! Yeah, right. "The Mystery of the Missing Backpack" or "The Secret of the Second Floor Bathroom." I wish! At least there would be a reason.

I know that my parents think I don't care, but it's not true. I... screw up a lot. When I sit down to do my homework, there is so much stuff I'd rather be doing. And when my Mom tries to "remind" me and "help" me, it just makes me mad! If she really wants to "help" me she should do the stupid homework!

So, I didn't have my ~~Social St~~ American History 1 essay done. Mrs. Ward was not pleased. Big surprise. That woman hates me. I guess I would hate me, too, if I were her. Fortunately, I'm not.

And, I didn't have my Outline for my Art Project. No comment.

Then, lunch.

In the Cafetorium today — could they possibly have come up with a lamer name? Cafetorium? Last week Jake and I were Wikipedia-ing, and came across "Vomitorium." Of course, we thought that was the funniest thing in the universe. So now, whenever anyone says something gross or stupid, we grab our stomachs and announce, "Where's the VOMITORIUM? I NEED THE VOMITORIUM!"

VOMITORIUM

It doesn't mean "a place to vomit" like we thought. But every time I hear that stupid word, Cafetorium, that's all I can think of.

So, in the Cafetorium today, the **only** person I know who was NOT "acting inappropriately" as Mrs. Wolfsteiger reported, was ME! But who gets sent to the office? You guessed it — ME!

Franklin was being his usual idiot self (pretty funny, actually), Jake was just — being Jake — and I was trying to eat my lunch. Franklin pantses Jake, Jake turns around, I say one little tiny thing, and I GET SENT TO THE OFFICE, AGAIN!

Our boneheaded Principal, Dr. German (or The Big G, as I call him) is in there. Sometimes, you catch a break and he's out prowling the halls, peeking in the classroom windows. He's a pretty creepy guy.

My science teacher, Mr. Rollins', wife made curtains to hang over the window in his classroom. Too cool. I love that guy! One day we were in science watching a movie and Mr. Rollins went over to the door and whipped it open, and Dr. German fell in! Mr. Rollins says, totally serious, "May I help you, sir?" Sir!

It was totally hilarious.

We just couldn't stop laughing. He got all "Hmmph" and really red in the face and went all funny fast-walking down the hall. Mr. Rollins was trying so hard not to laugh, but he was shaking all over and tears were just streaming out of his eyes. It was so awesome! I have no idea what the movie was about. Mr. Rollins just gave us all A's for the day and gave up trying to teach.

So now, every time I see Dr. German, all I can picture is him falling into the science room and doing that little crab walk down the hall. And, **I** know that **He** knows that's what I'm thinking.

So, I try just not to look at him. When I do, I laugh. I can't help it. I'm not trying to be mean or disrespectful. I can't control it. If I even **think** about him, I crack up.

So, I go to the office, and I'm standing there trying not to laugh — which is really hard and will get me into even MORE trouble — and Dr. German...The Big G...goes, "Ah, Maxwell. Again. Perhaps we should consider naming a small room in the basement after you. We could call it the Maxwell Pierce Detention Room."

Way to go, Big G. Real Funny Guy.

Maxwell Pierce memorial Detention Room

CHAPTER FIVE:

The Trouble With Maxwell

Pul-eeze!

Matilda's
Journal

Matilda

October 5 — Journal Entry #21

There were so many amazingly, fabulously great things that happened to *moi* today, that I don't know where to begin. Seriously, there was only one completely overarching (bigger than, embracing, or overshadowing everything) event that happened today: Jake sat next to me at lunch!!! More than just there's-a-space-so-I'll-just-crash-here, he had to push his way between me and Astrid, and then it was obvious that it wasn't Astrid that he wanted to be with. Thank you, thank you universe! JAKE LIKES ME!!!

It was especially cool, because he didn't make up some lame excuse, like, "I need to talk to you about the math homework" or something. He just put his tray down, said, "Excuse me, Astrid. Mind if I sit here?" sat down, looked at me, smiled, and said, ever so coolly, "Hi, Matilda." OMG!!!

He is so cute. I mean, OMG! if he were any cuter, he'd be a girl. That doesn't sound exactly the way I mean it. There's nothing girlie about him — he's just so…beautiful…in a TOTALLY boy way!

Of course, Matilda, Queen of Cool, couldn't think of one single thing to say. I mean: I stammered, I yammered, I went on and on about NOTHING. I could feel my face getting hot — and blushing!! OMG! It was so ~~overarch~~ absolutely humiliating. I SO wanted to just disappear…like vaporize…Beyond Hope! I am so pathetic.

Then Jake, gorgeous, funny, completely perfect Jake, says, "Did I tell you about the llama that got sleepy in school?"

He is so wonderful.

Why do these boys spend all their time on YouTube looking up stupid llama jokes???

But…I am seriously concerned about my best friend in the whole world…Maxwell, of course. He is starting to pass the "getting detention because he's so clueless and cute" stage. He's moving into the "dumb kids who spend their lives in detention and end up losers!" stage. What is the deal with him? He just doesn't seem to care if he gets known as a bad, lazy loser-ish kid! What about me?

Am I supposed to be the best friend of someone like that?

Anywho, for the last week, Maxwell has been showing up with *all his homework done…neatly…and on time!!!* Now, I grant you that would not be big news if we were talking about a highly clever and highly motivated person— such as mOi. **But…** this is *Maxwell* of whom we are speaking.

To add to this mysterious phenomenon
(fact, event, trend), we had a project due
in ~~Soc~~ American History 1 on Monday. I was
at Maxwell's *all* day on Sunday, and he didn't
even know what TOPIC he was going to do it
on!!! He was seriously stressed, but every
time I'd suggest something, he'd just laugh
it off or say, "Give it up!" or something.

BOYS!

We played foosball, and you'd've thought
the fate of the planet depended on it! I let
him win…although I am seriously fierce at
foosball.

I was totally, massively concerned about
his lack-of-project-progress. Maxwell is
one of the smartest people I know, so I
just don't get the homework thing…he's not
actually lazy…when he's really interested
in something he can, like, concentrate and

work for hours. (Of course, the things he's interested in are severely lame.) But, he doesn't try to get *out* of work (like I do... especially at home), and he finishes what he starts, usually.

Don't get me wrong. This is what I think about homework: it's a totally boring waste of time, so do it as fast as you can and don't worry about it. There are a lot of more interesting things to do than homework.

Dope!

If your homework gets handed in — even if it's mostly wrong or sloppy or not just perfect — it might take your grade down a little. Is that more important than finding out what's happening on your favorite soap? I think not. A−, B+, whatever. You'll still make High Honors.

And, only Total Nerds get straight A's: therefore, if you want to be cool, you have

to be careful about being TOO perfect with your schoolwork.

The exception is when there are PROJECTS due. Even though I do put them off (I put off *doing* them), I always know what I'm going to do, and I make sure that my Mom gets to the "Open 24 Hours" drugstore for the supplies before they close at midnight. She always yells at me, "Matilda, you've had **weeks** to do this and you're just starting it **NOW**?" She makes such a big deal out of everything — the drugstore is only, like, 15 or 20 minutes away!

But about Maxwell. His planner is a mess; his backpack is a mess; his folders are all messes. He loses **EVERYTHING.** He doesn't remember what he's supposed to do, and has the attention span of a flea. Do fleas actually have an attention span?

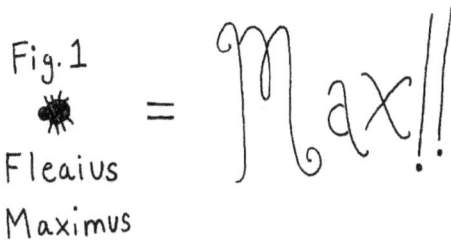

Fig. 1

✹ = Max!!

Fleaius Maximus

How would we measure it? Use teeny–weeny sensors behind dogs' ears????

I saw this program on the Discovery Channel — or some channel — about Stupid Studies the Government has spent like Trillions of dollars on that have no use in real life. Maybe somebody has already run an exhaustive (full, complete, in–depth) study of this flea–attention–span thing. Gosh! I sincerely hope so! Inquiring minds blah…blah…blah.

Back to Maxwell. Half the time he leaves his books in school. And he forgets his backpack in the **strangest** places. Do not get me started. They often have **urinals** in them. Yuk!

Urinal. That word needs to go on the Naughty Word List (NWL). I definitely think that **rectify** does, too. There are some words that just sound gross. But — just because they offend (upset, insult, rub–the–wrong–way) Ma Mere is no reason **NOT** to include them on the Naughty Word List. Rub–the–wrong–way needs to on the NWL, too.

The problem with/about/concerning Maxwell is: I don't think **he** does his homework. I think his mother does. It's going to — sooner or later — bite him on the butt. Teachers will find out, and then he's toast. I noticed Mrs. Ward when he handed in his Project to her. She had a look on her face — it was…thoughtful. It was like she was putting the pieces together. I think she knew that he hadn't done it, but she didn't want to bust him on it. Why???

OMG! My mother is becoming a serious nag! She comes into my room — where I have been writing in my Homework Journal for

hours! — and finds me texting Astrid. Like,
for one teensy weensy minute, I take a
break, and she has to come in RIGHT THEN.

RING!
RING!

Step away from the
phone!

Then, she's all like, "Matilda. If you're
just up here texting your friends and not
doing your homework — as you told me you
were — then I suggest that you *apply yourself*

to the cleaning of this room. It gives the term *pigsty* new meaning. If you are unable to do that, then you'll have to lose your phone for the rest of the week. A well-ordered work area indicates a well-ordered mind."

OINK!
OINK!

Where does she come up with these totally lame sayings?

Now, in all fairness, Ma Mere is a very intelligent woman. She is a voracious (insatiable, avid, greedy) reader and she writes a column that gets published in newspapers.

Anywho, my mother is very smart — in some areas.

But, lately, she's all over me about my room, leaving my stuff on the floor, etc., etc. So she goes, "Matilda, my dear, your room is a disaster. Remember: clean your room, or lose the phone."

Pul-eeze! She won't take my phone; she'll just yell at me. Then she'll give me the silent treatment.

I know…I'll put the dishes in the dishwasher tonight. That will make her happy.

Oh, wait. The Glitter Girls Go to Cooking Class is on tonight. Well, I'll put **my** dishes in the dishwasher — if they're not too yucky.

Astrid's calling.

adios,
matilda

CHAPTER SIX:

There Is Seriously Nothing to Like About School!

Maxwell's Journal

Maxwell

October 26

This has been a very weird week. Actually, it's been a weird couple of weeks.

Progress Reports came out a couple of weeks ago. So Daffy Duck, she's not that fat, but she waddles and her totally lame real name is Daphne Mallard. So, she writes this big essay about my potential, and not taking my work seriously, and other stuff. All my teachers wrote basically the same thing: doesn't hand in homework, not working up to his potential, lacks initiative, loser, doomed to be rejected by every college and have a miserable life; might as well just end it now and spare himself years of frustration.

How do *they* know what my potential is, anyway? Is it tattooed on my butt: POTENTIAL 9.7? So frustrating!

Seriously people, if you know the stuff, why do you have to do homework? And Projects? Is this just a teachers-trying-to-look-like-they're-important thing?

Finchley: English. The man is a moron. Why do I have to write reports and essays on moronic topics just to prove...what? That I can read? That I can think? And why does he care? I get A's on all my tests — get a life!

Mrs. Carpenter-Fincke: Language Arts. Imagination of a potato. Two words, BORE — ING.

Daffy Duck: Math. I get it, already. Doing 5 pages a night doesn't make me *understand it better* it makes me **hate it more**! Mostly it's a stupid, pointless waste of time, so I forget to bring my books or I lose my stuff. It's frustrating, and it makes the teacher mad at me. Then any little thing I do, I get detention.

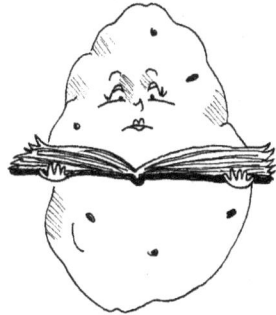

Unlike Franklin, your friendly neighborhood psycho, who never gets caught doing *anything* — because he does his homework and kisses up to the teachers.

PSYCHOPATH

Last Friday, Franklin brings in some of his Dad's old Mad Magazines. They are seriously warped. So we're looking at them — we sit in the back row so it's not like we're bothering anyone — and he shows me this cartoon. You know how sometimes you just see something and it's so funny you can't help yourself? So, Daffy asks a question, I guess, and no one answers her, and I see this cartoon, and I just…explode. I'm trying NOT to laugh, so it gets

all bottled up inside, but it's so HILARIOUS,
that it just comes out all at once. I
laughed really loud, spit, stuff coming out
my nose, hiccupping, crying, can't breathe
totally helpless laughing. Franklin is trying
to take the (now wet and disgusting snotty
magazine) off my desk before Daffy sees it,
I am helpless, now all the other kids are
laughing, and Daffy looks like
her head is going to explode. I
don't even wait; I just get up
and go to the office.

Franklin, as usual, skates. I
don't get it. The kid NEVER gets
in trouble!

Mrs. Ward: American History
1. Now there's a…mystery. She
should hate me, and I think
she did. Now I don't think she
hates me. I don't know what
she thinks. History was never my favorite,
but she makes it…fun. She's actually a good

teacher, and she brings in these really funny cartoons. I don't know where she gets them. It's always only me and Matilda who think they're funny — and they really are funny, just not funny in the usual way.

Matilda says they're for smart people, which is why we are the only two who appreciate them. I don't know about that, but I do know that they crack me up.

Then when I laugh, Franklin makes kissy sounds.

I don't kiss up. They're funny, and she's smart, and I like her. There! I said it! I like Mrs. Ward, and I'm SO sorry that I fell for that stupid joke the first day of school. If I knew — for sure — who set me up, I'd seriously

I LIKE MRS. WARD!

hurt him — or her. It was mean, and I'm not mean. I might be stupid, but I'm not mean.

Mrs. Ward's note on the Report did say, *missing homework*, but that was all. She could have said a lot worse. The only one who didn't comment was Mr. Rollins, my science teacher. I love science, and he is a great teacher. I always do my homework for his class because:

1. It's interesting.

2. He doesn't give a lot of it.

3. He calls me "the mad scientist" because I'm always coming up with weird uses for things.

4. He's a really cool guy.

5. He hates Dr. German: The Big G.

6. I've got an A+ in that class.

So, after my parents read the Report from The Dark Side, as Austin called it, they scheduled me for an appointment with some doctor. I'm supposed to go next week, I think.

Now I'm really worried.

1. Austin is being nice to me. He is "helping" me with my homework. Actually, he is doing my homework. *Am I dying?*

2. Mom and Dad are being unusually nice to me. Instead of ragging on me — like they have since first grade — about my homework, they're making excuses for me — and doing it for me. Not writing it, but like looking over my shoulder and telling me what to say, or correcting an answer. Mom pretty much did my whole American History 1 Project. I'm sure

Mrs. Ward smelled a rat, but she didn't say anything.

   3. They made this appointment with a doctor.

   4. I'm scared.

I HATE SCHOOL.

   Oh, Gym. All last year, I got an A+ in Gym. But nobody cared about that. Now, I got a **Progress Report** — about Gym. I forgot my Gym clothes like 10 times, so I had to sit out. I'm such a **FAIL**!

   I need to talk to Matilda.

CHAPTER SEVEN

I
L-O-V-E
Jake!!!

Pul-eeze!

Matilda's Journal

Matilda

—MEMO—

From the desk of Augustus P. Reilly, Ed.D.
Chichester County Superintendent of Schools

Dear Students and Parents:

As we prepare for the beautiful holiday — Thanksgiving — we remember our ancestors, those brave men and women who fought unthinkable hardships to found a free colony in the New World. Yet, we must not forget about the annual event which occurs every January: The All-State Science Fair. In past years, Chichester County School students have always exhibited winning entries. Last year, however, Chichester students did not place in the top 3 for any category. Shame on us! This year, I fully expect that our students and their parents will rise to the challenge. Then, we will have even more for which to be thankful.

OMG! I swear, this man stays up at night, writing these missives (letter, note, memo) purely for my entertainment. This one is especially delicious! Can't you just smell it? That's the scent of butt-kissing!!

First, thank you SO MUCH for reminding me that the holiday is named Thanksgiving. That one's always been a real challenge for me!

And the unthinkable hardships:

1. If they're truly **unthinkable,** then how can he write about them? Oh! That must mean that **he doesn't** *think when he writes these moronic notes!*

2. Does he mean they didn't have cable? No Satellite? No "Glamour Girls See The World"? WOW! That is hardship!

Glamour Girls See The World ☆

3. And, if they're unthinkable — let's not think about them, Gus.

Next: love the reminder of the *real* meaning of "annual." For those of us who have experienced the pain and humiliation of permanent brain freeze, "annual" means "every year" or — in this case — every January. Not every other January, or every-once-in-a-while in January, but every single one. **Whew!** Thanks, A–Gus–Tush, for clearing that up!

TERMINAL BRAIN FREEZE

Then we come to the part about student exhibitionists. If I were Gus, I would not wish to speak publicly about that. (I had to look it up. **OMG!** This is SO-0-0-0 nasty!!! I am certainly not going to write

about THOSE DIRTY THINGS
in my Homework Journal!)
Shame on **YOU**, Gus-Gus!!!!

But, the best, the
real Beauty Part, is the
oh-so-subtle **HINT** to the
parents: our students
and their parents will rise to the challenge.
Does this guy really think that we have no
functioning brain matter at all? That we won't
all understand that instructing the parents
to "help" is code for: Do Your Kid's Science
Project In Spite Of The Rules Which Forbid It!

What a lame brain! I mean, am I the only
one who finds that insulting? Like, we are
so inept (clumsy, useless, hopeless) that
we kids can't even come up with our own
projects?

That man gives
butt-kissing a
bad name! What
a miserable

Ultimate butt Kissing!

Matilda's Journal

hypocrite — louse — creepy — crawly — skuzzy…
well, you get the idea. I **DO NOT** like him. At
all. He's just…**NOT** a nice person.

Anywho, when I was expressing my
displeasure with the previously mentioned
epistle (oh, did it already; same as missive,
means MEMO), lovely Jake came over and asked
me — ME — if I want to be his partner for
the Science Fair!!!!! LOVE IS IN BLOOM!

When I texted Astrid and Alyssa, they
both texted back, "No way!" so I replied
"Way!" and they said, "NO WAY!" and I said,

"YES! WAY!!!" And they…well, they were incredulous (doubtful, uncertain, unsure). Probably also a teensy weensy bit jealous.

Things I LOVE–ADORE–WORSHIP about Jake!

• The way his hair kind of falls over his ~~left no, right,~~ I need a mirror – right eye. Too cute.

• The super-cute striped shirts he always wears. What are they called? Oh, yeah…T-shirts with collars. Nice.

• AND – he wears shorts in the WINTER, which I totally love!!!!

All hail King Jake!

More Things I LOVE-ADORE-WORSHIP about Jake!

- He smells good.
- He's smart, but not show-offy.
- He thinks **WWIT** is stupid!!!!!
- He thinks Maxwell is smart.
- He likes Max's llama jokes — which are

SO stupid, but I like them, too.

So, I am deeply in love (not "in like,"

like Alyssa says, which NO ONE says

anymore).

Very excited about my dance recital.

Should I invite Jake???? What if he says

"no"? What if he says "yes," but then doesn't

come?? What if he comes, but thinks it's

stupid?? Are there aliens??? Matilda! Get a

grip!

Peace + Love,
Matilda ☮

CHAPTER EIGHT:

Will the Real Maxwell Stand Up? Not You, Loser!

Maxwell's Journal

Maxwell

There are no words to describe what a mess I am in. None.

Tomorrow, I will be out of school. I have an appointment with Dr. P., and his office is in the city.

Today, I got called down to the Guidance Office. Getting called to Guidance stinks just as much as being sent the Principals office. Plus, they announce it on the loud speaker so everyone looks at you when you leave class.

He showed me a copy of my Report Card that my parents will get today. I got 1 A-, 2 C's, 3 D's, and I failed — Gym! I am now on **Academic Suspension**!

ACADEMIC
SUSPENSION

Because of the suspension, I can't play basketball for the quarter. By the time the quarter's over, the season will be almost over, and Coach probably won't play me anyway. It wouldn't be fair to the guys who went to every practice and every game.

Then he asked me a whole bunch of creepy questions about my parents and stuff. What a geek! It was awful.

But — probably not as awful as what's been going on at my house since last week.

And — probably not as awful as what's going to happen when I get home today.

Or as majorly awful as what will happen tomorrow at that doctor's!

Okay. Here's what happened. Last week — Wednesday? Thursday? Who keeps track? — I came home without my math book or my LA book. Wait...it was Thursday.

MISSING
LA
MATH
CALL MAXWELL

We had a lot of math homework, and a quiz the next day. For LA, we were supposed to read a really long, really boring essay — and then answer a bunch of stupid, boring, nobody-cares-about questions.

BORING.

Well, I wasn't too bugged about leaving my stuff in school, because I do it all the time. I figured I probably could get a note from my Mom if I asked her — begged her — so that I wouldn't get detention and get benched. I'd probably flunk the math quiz, but I could make that up. And Austin would help me with the LA assignment on the weekend.

Turns out, Mom was talking to Matilda's Mom, so she knew about the quiz, and the homework, and my detentions, and that Matilda had told her Mom that I hadn't done my ~~Socia~~ American History 1 project — Mom had.

My Mom was REALLY angry. I have never seen her so **MAD.** Usually, she is pretty cool about stuff, and we joke around a lot about the dumb homework,

YIKES!

and she ends up helping me, or Austin does, or Dad does, and so — about half of the time — I have homework to hand in. I don't see what the big problem is.

But my Mom was ripped! She did the "Wait until your Father Gets Home" thing — Oh, Man! I haven't heard that one since the first grade!

When he got home, we had this big Family Meeting. Even Austin. My parents were saying how they tried to help me, but I didn't care about trying; I wasn't responsible; I blew off my work, blah, blah, blah.

Actually, it made me feel pretty bad about myself. I don't see myself that way.

Okay. I, Maxwell:

- Am a good kid

- Rock at basketball, soccer and baseball

- Am a funny guy

- I'm well-liked — no brag

- Have a lot of friends

- Don't get in trouble…

Oh…I AM in trouble.

Big trouble.

Even Austin was mad at me. He can be a real moron, sometimes, but he usually ends up on my side. He said he thought I just didn't care enough to try and be organized; that he tried to help me, but that I was just turning into — A SLACKER. That word — SLACKER.

SLACKER

Gosh! Who are these people and why are they all being so mean to me?

I called Matilda. My best friend. She said she was worried. That kids were starting to talk — like how I was getting in trouble more than was cool. Then she started talking about Jake...and her mother being after her about doing homework and cleaning her room...

AND SHE DIDN'T EVEN KNOW ABOUT THE ACADEMIC SUSPENSION. NO ONE DID.

WHAT WILL HAPPEN WHEN THEY FIND OUT?

Is it all over for me? Am I just going to be that guy who used to be kind of cool but turned into a loser? Will I get switched out of all my AP classes into classes where I have no friends? Do I still HAVE any friends?

What have I been doing? Austin says my work ethic stinks. My teachers say I'm disorganized and sloppy. My parents say I have no study skills.

What if they're all right? What have I

been doing? Austin says I just quit when I have to do hard work...homework. He says that I just do what I like, and blow off everything else.

I don't think that's fair. I always do my science homework. I'm good at science. I just *happen* to like science. Oh. I am so busted.

The world is poo.

I HATE talking on the phone.

Oh, Man!

Call Matilda.

CHAPTER NINE:

Why Are Boys So Dumb??????

Pul-eeze!

Matilda's
Journal

Matilda

I am such a good friend. Seriously!

OMG! I have been on my phone — plugged

 in, because the battery ran down — that's how long I've been talking to the kid! — for hours! He's FREAKING OUT!

I told Maxwell to go make himself a big bowl of popcorn and then call me back. He was a little calmer. That's another thing about boys. They're simple like goldfish. Just feed them, and they feel better.

So, anyway, after he was back in bed, munching, I reminded him about Astrid in the third grade. How she was always in trouble and crying and throwing stuff and her papers all looked like they were scribbled by a crazy llama.

CRAZY LLAMA!

Maxwell said the only thing he remembered about third grade was that our teacher, Mrs. Donald, used to bring in homemade cookies every Friday. See? I rest my case. Boys! (They *were* good cookies.) But at least he laughed at the llama part.

Maxwell thinks he has problems? He's a Space Shot — total Star Wars Freak-o! He's just a dolt. Astrid has problems! **Astrid has ADHD. So do six other kids in my grade.**

Back to the third grade. Franklin used to call her "Astrid the Disaster." She could never find anything, she was ALWAYS having to be told, "Astrid, no talking, dear" and "Astrid, please return to your seat, dear" and "Astrid, are you sure your paper isn't in your folder, dear?" I guess in elementary school, when they yell at you, it's obligatory (compulsory, mandatory, required, you have to) to use the word "dear." Even if

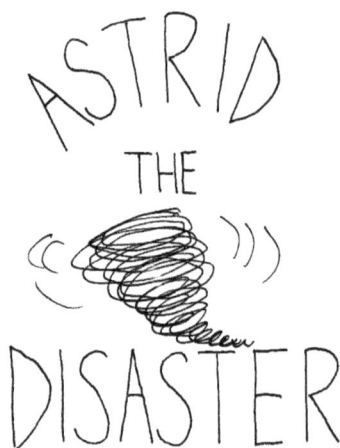

they said "dear," she usually had at least
one meltdown/hissy fit per day.

Anywho, her parents also took her to
Dr. P., and she loved him. Now she's totally
cool…AND, she gets to use a laptop in
school all the time because her handwriting
is really bad — which I don't understand,
because the girl
is a GENIUS at
drawing. Her
cartoons are so
good — I swear,
she could get
them published.

Llamas in Love
by Astrid

My mother even says so! Anywho, she takes
some kind of medicine in the morning, which
really chills her out and helps her to focus.
I can always tell when she has forgotten
to take her meds — she is a **COMPLETE** (in
the real, not-Maxwell-like way) Space Shot:
disorganized, forgetful, talks ALL THE TIME
NON-STOP, interrupts ALL the time and you

can be right in the middle of a serious discussion, when she will start talking about some random thing.

It is seriously annoying.

Like yesterday, we were eating lunch, and Alyssa was telling us about her brother, who got in a car wreck and was really upset (Alyssa, not her brother, though he probably IS upset, since he's in the hospital *with* a broken leg and *without* a **spleen** — whatever that is) (**spleen** goes on the Naughty Word List (NWL) — it sounds absolutely DISGUSTING!), and right in the middle Astrid

says, "Look at that cute little girl! Her shirt has sparkly things on it!" And I say, "Did you take your meds today?" And she says, "Um, no. I ran out and my mom has to refill it today. Why?"

Oooo Shiny!

She is all over the place when she forgets to take those meds. Anywho, Maxwell was just afraid to go to Dr. P. I told him Dr. P. can't be that bad — just look at Astrid. Also, her parents use some kind of system called **"What's the Rule?"** to help with homework. Hold On! Her mother was talking to my mother, and Ma Mere said something about **"What's the Rule?"** for me. Seriously?

Anywho, everyone knows that Maxwell needs HELP!

So, now it is sometime in the REALLY EARLY MORNING and I am sleepy. I think that Max is okay, *finally*!

He needs to see that getting some help is

A GOOD THING!

Good Night, Maxwell.

Seriously! Boys! They're all about their "image."

(OMG! I totally forgot to choose my outfit for tomorrow! I wonder what I should wear? Maybe my pink ruffled blouse — with the headband with the big, poufy flower? Hmmm. Or, the …)

Bon soir,
Matilda

CHAPTER TEN:

The Visit With Dr. P. WHAT A GUY!

Maxwell's Journal

Maxwell

November 17

Out of school today. Basically, it was a VERY GOOD DAY!

Dr. P. is cool. Surprise.

At first, it was a little weird. The whole family was there, even *Austin the Disloyal Skunk-Rat.*

AUSTIN
SKUNK RAT

So we're sitting in the car. Austin and I are both in the back seat. We're listening to our iPods and NOT looking at each other. Mom and Dad are in the front with big fake smiles on.

I am trying to be mature — for real! So I'm working hard to ignore Austin the Skunk-Rat. I'm determined not to act immature...not give him any clue of how revolting I think he is. Only...a couple of times I shoot him a look and hold my nose like **YOU STINK!**

YOU STINK!

Okay, maybe it was 3 or 4 times…6, tops.

But, Austin the Skunk-Rat **TOTALLY IGNORES ME!** It makes me ballistic. It's not that he's pretending to ignore me — he really is! It's like I don't even exist — right there, 20 inches from him, and it's like he's **ALONE.**

If I ever speak to him again, I have to find out how he does that.

It was a long ride.

So we get there, and the office is okay. My parents have been there before, and they are kind of proud. They're all, "See? We told you it would be good!" and I'm, "Yeah, right."

Truth: He has a Pool Table right in the Waiting Room. How cool is that? So, Austin the Skunk-Rat wants to play pool. No way was

I going to forgive him! He says, "You want to shoot some pool?" and I just shrug. No way will I give him the satisfaction of talking to him, that Skunk–Rat–Butthead.

Here's what happened. We shot some pool; I beat Austin — not with the pool cue, which I kept thinking about — but he scratched on the cue ball. Ha!

Then Dr. P. comes out and we all go in his office.

Truth: He has a Foosball Table right in his office. How cool is that?

He catches me looking at it, and he says, "How about a little one-on-one later? I'm pretty good at Foosball." So I say, "Yeah," and then we all just sit around and talk. Dr. P. asks a lot of questions, but,

SURPRISE!

NOT about loser Maxwell!

They're just about family stuff...when my mom was pregnant...what our schedules are like...and other boring things.

Then he sends them out, and him and me play Foosball. **HE IS VERY GOOD!** We played 3 games, and I only won 1. That was cool. I thought he'd be either:

1. Bad at it. He's pretty old. At least 40.

2. He'd let me win. That'd be lame. No kid likes that.

I was sweating from Foosball. Llama stink.

Llama stink!

Here's what happened. He asked me about my routine, my sports, stuff like that. It wasn't bad. He's a pretty funny guy; not lame, trying-to-get-on-the-good-side-of-the-kid-by-acting-all-cool like my soccer coach, Mr. Baransky, "Call me Mike"

Baransky. Not in this life, you tool.

He's just got one of those warped senses of humor. It was like talking to Matilda, if Matilda were old and had a beard.

VOMITORIUM!

Dr.P?

So, it was easy to talk to him. I had a feeling that he wasn't going to run out and squeal on me to my parents. So, I was pretty honest. I actually TRIED to be honest. I mean, I am in deep poop! So then – here is the amazing part – he brings my parents and skunk–rat–butthead back in, and he kind of lays it all ON THEM!

But not in a mean way.

Here's the important stuff: We are going to start doing something called, "What's the Rule?"

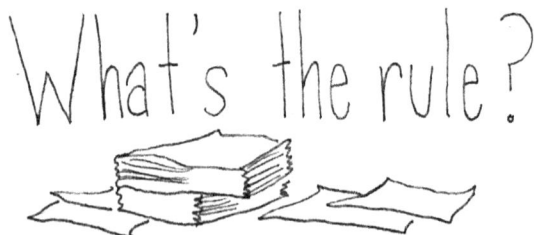

What's the rule?

1. Parents need to change their sloppy, irresponsible ways! *Okay. He didn't exactly say that, but I can read between the lines.*

2. Maxwell has TOO MUCH homework. *Well, yuh!*

3. Regular time for homework, BUT, he will work on homework for no more than one hour; if he can't finish, then he just STOPS! *How cool is that?*

4. Nobody interferes, nags, reminds, helps him (unless he asks for explanation). *Sweet!!! Oh…the no help part kind of stinks… but the no nagging or reminding part is good.*

5. Maxwell needs to be playing basketball! It is important that he…*has a life. You think? Go, Dr. P.!*

6. **What's the Rule?** means no TV, video games…during homework time. Pack backpack for next day. *No problem.*

7. Dr. P. will write a note to the school… blah blah blah…schedule review…time for

homework…blah blah blah…quiet place, kitchen, no distractions…*This guy could be my hero!*

8. And never — not even once — did he say that I was lazy, immature or irresponsible, or had a bad work ethic, etc. *So there, Austin, you skunk-rat-boogerhead!*

This totally rocks! His plan is so awesome for ME!

Texted Matilda; battery must be dead. Franklin was texting me all the way home — new llama jokes. Jake texted about game night.

I just left Dr. P.'s office, and already I'm back to being me. Sweet!

MAXWELL IS BACK!

CHAPTER ELEVEN:

OMG!
My Life Is Over
— Finished —
And a Total
Disaster!!

Pul-eeze!

Matilda's
Journal

Matilda

OMG! Today was **The Worst Day of My Life.** It's official. I am ruined. Not only did I:

- NOT make Honor Roll — ME!
- GET detention — ME! TWICE!
- GET yelled at by a teacher — ME!
- GET sent to the Principal's Office — ME!
- RUIN my pink ruffled blouse in Art — M
- NOW I AM GROUNDED. ME! **GROUNDED!**
- And — they took my PHONE away.

And — NO IM-ing.

Life is no longer worth living.

How can people **EXIST** without cell phones?? How can you live in total social isolation? How will I know if I am still THE MOST POPULAR GIRL AT CHICHESTER MIDDLE SCHOOL?????

My life is over!

RIP Matilda

OMG! OMG! OMG! OMG! OMG! OMG! OMG! OMG! OMG!

Okay. To start from the beginning.

We all know that I am very cool. For sure, my teachers — who all ganged up on me for no reason — need to appreciate that I am a social person! They do not seem to value my individuality and...coolness. I thought they did. BIG mistake.

I mean, really. They could have just **said something** like, "Matilda, you seem to be falling behind on your homework. It could affect your grade." Oh — Mrs. Ward actually did say that.

Well, like, "Matilda, your homework is so sloppy that I can't read it. If you want to get credit, you'll have to redo it all by the end of next week." Um — I think Ms. Mallard may have said something like

that, but Astrid was talking to me about…
something EXTREMELY important…although I
can't remember what it was…at the time, so I
was not, actually…paying attention.

And paying attention. What is this
not paying attention junk,
anyway? If they REALLY don't
want you to text, or write
notes, or — whatever, they
should make it a policy, tell
us, something! And since
when is taking notes in class mandatory
(necessary, a rule, enforced) anyway? Hmm.
Maybe *that* was what Mr. Rollins said…a few
times. Well, it's his fault if I didn't take
him seriously! He's too nice!

And if handing stuff in late is going to
bring you down **ONE WHOLE LETTER GRADE** they
should REALLY tell you! I mean, what is this,
like, "Let's just pull this little joke on
the kids? We'll just mark them down for late
work and keep it a secret??? I mean, that's

um, since when??

just not fair! Mrs. Carpenter–Fincke (that name is seriously weird — it's going on my NWL!!!) might have mentioned something like that, but who can understand her, anyway?

But Gym? GYM?? Like, not suiting up for gym is IMPORTANT????? My gym teacher "MS. EDDY" — ooh!!!!!

Here's what's wrong with **MS.** Eddy:

• First of all, it's **MS.** Eddy. And she says it like that. What's up with that?

• She has this really red face. It's, like, tomato red all the time. When I see her, I can't stop thinking about tomatoes.

• And SUCH bad hair! OMG! Don't even get me started about the hair! Does the word "scrubbing pad" describe it enough???

• She has **WWE muscles. Very** unattractive and scary.

• And — she's **MEAN!!!!**

• What could be a bigger sign that my life is ruined, than that I am stressing over MY GYM TEACHER!!!!

My Life Is Over!

Even if my parents would let me go to the dance, the school won't. What will Jake do? He'll be totally distraught (upset, troubled, panic-stricken). *poor Jake!*

1. So: my A's — went down to B's.

2. My B+'s — went down to B-'s

3. AND — OMG! This is so embarrassing! My B- went down to a **C-**!

A **C-** in Gym — and it actually counts!

Then I got detention — for not handing in my homework. And when I…protested (complained, griped, objected, whined, had a hissy fit!) I got **YELLED AT** by that mousy little woman, Mrs. Carpenter-Fincke!! Of all people…and then she gave me a SECOND detention. And then she sent me to the **PRINCIPAL'S OFFICE!!!** (Home of the NTD!!)

Dr. German wasn't even there!!! (Probably out

creeping around the halls.)
(That was the ONLY good
thing that happened today!)

PRINCIPAL'S OFFICE

The yucky part, of course, was that I was alone with the scary NTD. I just stayed as far away from it as I could, until the secretary told me to wait in the Guidance Office.

Mr. Coleman, the Guidance Counselor, sent me back to class. I got to Art REALLY late, and — of course — Olivia, **a.k.a.** WWIT had

WWIT

to be all like, "Ooh, poor Matilda! Are you all right? You look like you've been crying."

OOH! I had been, but I didn't want WWIT telling everyone. She's gonna get it from me! I was trying so hard not to cry in front of everyone. I felt my hands shaking, then I spilled that stupid papier mâché glop…all over my 4th favorite blouse. One more reason to HATE WWIT!

So, I get home, and my mother is waiting for me. She has gotten my Report Card. She is soooo MEAN to me! I feel really bad, and all she can do is YELL at me!

Does she feel bad for me that all my teachers STINK? NO!

Does she feel sorry that I got a bad report card — through no fault of my own? NO!

Is she even a teensy weensy bit sad that I had the humiliation of going to the Principal's Office (with the NTD!!!)? NO!

Or that I'm not allowed to go to the stupid Fall Frolic??? NO!

In fact, she says that, in her opinion, I didn't get punished enough!

But, she's willing to take care of that situation by

Grounding Me For The Rest of My Natural Life!!!

I really need to talk to Maxwell.

CHAPTER TWELVE:

Dr. P. WHAT A HUGE BOOGERHEAD!

Maxwell's Journal

Maxwell

December 13

This is so messed up, that I hardly know where to begin.

After we all saw Dr. P., my parents had this very cool take on stuff. They went in to the school, and basically got my homework situation straightened out. At least, that's what I thought! The deal was, do homework for an hour, then you're done.

So, I was doing my homework in the kitchen, like Dr. P. said. Mom is there, so she can help, if needed. Great. **EXCEPT:** My mom's job is cooking. So she's either making big pots of stuff or rolling dough or checking the oven 50 times a second or talking on the phone about making pots of stuff or rolling dough or needing to check the oven.

So, she said I had to do my homework in my room, not the family room or kitchen or basement. Too many **distractions**.

That's okay. My room is good. I have a desk and my laptop and my iPod and my phone and my PSP, and all my stuff. I can't use my stuff during homework time, of course. So, I don't. Except in emergencies—which happen a lot.

Emergency!

For the first couple of days, Mom was sort of "hovering," but then she and Dad saw Dr. P. again, and she stopped. Austin just walked by a few times and made the "get going" sign — pointing at me and giving me his eyebrows-up, mouth-all-squinched-up weird look — but he stopped, too.

So, I'm cruising along, doing a few math problems, part of an essay, ALL my science — I do that first — and most of whatever

I have to do for AH1. I check the clock a
lot; I don't want to work for over an hour,
because that's *unnecessary*, says Dr. P.

We had this follow-up meeting with him,
and went over my schedule. "The Rule" was
that I do homework after dinner between
7:30 and 8:30. That way, I
can go to basketball practice
YEAH! (yeah!), get showered,
hang with my friends,
have dinner. In other
words, have a life. Then one
hour of homework, pack my backpack, then
whatever until bedtime.

I have a planner book, and my teachers
put my homework assignments in it.

If I need help, I can ask my parents, but
they can't do my work. I decided that I don't
need help. Whenever I ask, I get a long
explanation for whatever it is, and it is too
BORING. Why can't they just use three or four

word sentences then stop?

Anyway, Dr. P. made it clear that my schoolwork is **MY RESPONSIBILITY**. So, okay. I've got less work, I've got sports back. I can do this.

This is how I was thinking, and everything was SO GREAT!!! I mean, no hassles at home, no hassles at school…what could be better? And then Progress Notes came out.

I am failing
everything!!!!!!
EVERY SINGLE CLASS!!!!!!
SERIOUSLY?
My Life is over!

That Dr. P. is a dumbbutt. How could he do this to me? I thought everything was going great. I was doing **exactly** what he said.

1. Working like crazy for one full hour. Okay, sometimes I maybe didn't do the whole

hour. I got some calls and texts that were important — like, Jake needs me to bring my World of Warriors game to his house on Friday — he got a new system and we link up! Or — everybody understands this — before school, I was just about to beat Level 12 — the last level — on Temples of Destruction. I HAD to finish it! Homework time was the first time I had all day. It took about 30 seconds; no big deal.

2. Anyway, **ONLY** one hour of homework? Who can sit and concentrate for one whole hour? Okay. I admit. It sounded pretty good when he talked about it. I mean, I'd been sitting trying to do homework sometimes for 2 or 3 or 4 hours, so one hour sounded great. But one hour is **60 minutes!**

3. Then there's the "getting ready" thing. Part of **What's the Rule?** is that I have my backpack organized and bring home everything I

....Ready?

need and take it all back to school the next day. That's okay. I have to have my backpack ready to go before I can watch my programs — at night, after homework time, before bedtime. A couple of times I forgot, so no Star Wars that night. Now I remember.

4. Of course, what goes in the backpack is ~~suposed~~ supposed to be finished homework, or at least a reasonable sample of homework for each class. I did this — mostly… sometimes.

5. Getting my homework assignments filled in by my teachers. Okay. This is where it gets…not good.

LAME.

It's really lame to be hanging around after class, waiting for your teacher to write in your book. I feel like it's first grade all over again. I had to make up excuses to stay behind, and it got embarrassing so I stopped. Not the excuses, the waiting and

getting the book filled in. But **I know** what
I have to do! I don't need some teacher
writing in a little book! I always know.
Okay, I usually get it right. Often. Maybe I
mess up sometimes…and then I don't have the
right books or papers…or know that a honkin
big project was due for LA.

6. Maybe I am a total **LOSER**.

But it's all Dr. P.'s fault,
with his, "This is Maxwell's
responsibility. You have it set up
for him, and now it's up to him."

Set up is right.

I have been set up
By Dr. P.
And my parents
TO FAIL!

I miss Matilda. What is going on with her
Mother?

CHAPTER THIRTEEN:

What's the Rule? You Crazy Fool!!!

Pul-eeze!

Matilda's Journal

Matilda

—MEMO—

From the desk of Augustus P. Reilly, Ed.D.
Chichester County Superintendent of Schools

Dear Students and Parents:

As the season of perpetual joy and hope comes upon us, whether we celebrate with a menorah or an evergreen, we must not forget about the annual event which occurs every January: The All-State Science Fair. In past years, Chichester County School students have always exhibited winning entries. Last year, however, Chichester students did not place in the top 3 for any category. Shame on us! This year, I fully expect that our students and their parents will rise to the challenge! May this season bring all of you hope, joy and peace.

OMG! Now he's recycling his inspiring notes. His creepy communiqués (letter, note, memo). What a complete TOOL!!!

Okay. Menorah or evergreen? Pul-eeze!!!

So, just in case we (stupid silly kids – SSK's) were even THINKING of doing our own projects, he has to write ANOTHER boneheaded memo to remind the parents to **"help"** with the projects. WHAT A CREEP!!!!!!!

And…He smells. All right. Maybe this is mean, but it's true. He does smell. My Mom and I were picking my Dad up from a school meeting, and A–Gus–Tush comes out with my Dad, and he comes over to the car and he sticks his head in and his scarf goes flying in my face and it smells like…wet dog…and…

NASTY old sneakers...and school Cafetorium trash bins...and... Ooh, ugh! Gross out! **Nasty!**

Anywho, he smells icky. AND he sticks his head, like, All The Way In The Window — **right in my face** — which would be scary even if he didn't say anything or smell bad because he has a lot of hair growing out of places you usually don't want hair growing (like your nose... EEEUW!!!) and he has on this strange-looking beret (round soft hat) — and he says (and he has this mint candy thing in his mouth that he's sucking on, and it looks like a **moving tooth!!!**), "Greetings, Matilda. It's nice to see you in more salubrious" (decent,

Greetings Matilda!

...SHM!

healthy, respectable — I had to look it up) "circumstances!"

He really talks like that. Even my Dad was laughing, and all night kept saying stuff like, "Be certain to keep yourself in SA-LUB-RI-OUS circumstances, Matilda!" or, "Matilda, avoid detention and other non-SA-LUB-RI-OUS environments!" which was, actually, pretty funny, except that Ma Mere gets all scrunchy-faced whenever she remembers my detention and not-so-good grades.

Ma Mere has instituted (set up, started, introduced) **What's the Rule?** for homework. Sigh!

Soo-o-o-o, the thing is, that I have to do my homework in the kitchen, at 5:00 PM, for about an hour. I show Ma Mere the planner, and I decide how to do it, like, in what order…so, I do the easiest stuff first, and then the harder (**a.k.a.** boring!) last. So, I will admit that I sometimes doodle (I just love that word; it's so Cute! Doodle

— doodle — doodle — don't you think that sounds adorable?) on my papers — ANYTHING to not have to think about the boring-stuff-that-I-don't-like!!!

And then, after a while, I am too tired to do the easy-stuff-that-I-should-have-done-first.

At first, Ma Mere said that **The Rule** was that homework time was 7:00 PM to 8:00 PM. That was a **DISASTER!**

Glitter Girls is on at 8:00 PM, and I have to get ready for it. I **ALWAYS** watch Glitter Girls in my P.J.'s, with my Pillow Pet (that's my thing — don't ask me why, don't tell ANYONE I do this, it's SO LAME!), and I have my favorite snack — instant hot chocolate with those shortbread cookie things (those are the rectangle shaped ones that look like they took a fork and mushed it cross-wise on the top of the cookie). I prefer to eat 4 of those with my hot chocolate. Occasionally (rarely, irregularly, every once in a while) Ma Mere forgets to buy the right cookies, so I have to "make do" ("Make due???"...one of Ma Mere's little sayings) with chocolate chip.

So, you can see...I don't like to just, you know, RUSH away from the kitchen table and QUICKLY throw my favorite snack together and RUN to my room to change and grab my you-know-what (Pillow Pet...Shhh!), and then be in front of the TV by 8:00 PM. **Whew!**

There were a couple of tense nights: spilled my hot chocolate on the couch (yellow) and the rug (white) and **MYSELF!** Forgot my you-know-what so I had nothing to hug — my cat, Oliver, is SO not into hugging.

Not good. So Ma Mere, while cleaning the carpet, said we should move homework time to 5:00 PM. I am home from dance or gymnastics by then, so it seemed better. Less messy. And the chocolate stained my favorite lavender P.J.s with the purple bows and the little hearts made out of lace! Extremely sad.

So, **The Rule** is: Homework at 5:00 PM. Then, at 6:00 PM — or earlier, if I finish earlier, which mostly actually happens, then I can read.

Okay. It took…a while…for me to get with the program. "Get with the program, Matilda!" as my mother said, *many times.*

Because — let's face it! — someone like ME does NOT want to labor (work, toil, struggle — ESPECIALLY struggle!) on homework.

I mean, Pul—eeze!!! It's homework. It's SO
not important.

   And what difference did it make if it's
a little…messy. Or, not perfectly correct…
all the time. I mean, if
I could read it, and I
really DO understand it
— I was just in a hurry —
then what's the big deal,

AS IF!

right?

   I showed Ma Mere my essay for LA, because
I thought it was really excellent. She said
it was good, but hard to read. She *suggested*
that if I wrote it more neatly,
I might get an **A.** "Matilda,
what's the point in **DOING** it if
no one can **READ** it?"

HUH??

   Actually…I REALLY hate to
say this…she has a point. It
does stink to get marked down
because THEY CAN'T READ IT!!! That is just
so wrong…but, I digress (go off the point,

wander). I heard that on Glitter Girls last night — I think it sounds seriously Cool!!!

So, I got with the program. Anywho, if I am totally honest: **What's the Rule?** is not that bad. So, I do my homework neatly, I pay attention in class…mostly…and I am back to A's.

Except, when Progress Reports came out, my parents got one, and I was ABSOLUTELY PANICKED! until my mother said, "Matilda! You did it! Straight A's! I am so **PROUD** of you."

WOW! Straight A's! That is so totally ~~terrific~~ TERRIBLE! OMG!

Now **everyone** will think I'm a NERD!!!!!

MAXWELL!!!!!!

PS: Hanging out in the kitchen with my Mom while I do my homework is actually kind of nice.

NERD??

PPS: Jake and I are doing **OUR** Science Project **by ourselves.** It may not be all that great…but, who cares? I'm doing it

WITH JAKE!!!

PPPS: Winning isn't everything, you know. Grow up!

Grow up!

yours truly,
#1 Matilda

CHAPTER FOURTEEN:

Not Totally Bad!

Maxwell's Journal

Maxwell

Life does not completely stink! And I owe it all to:

- Dr. P.

- Mrs. Ward

- Astrid

- Austin

- My parents, who turned out to be pretty cool!

- Matilda, who is the BEST friend anybody ever had.

But, before my life got better, it got a LOT **WORSE**!

The Progress Reports were rough. It seemed like I was doing the right stuff...but I guess NOT. So we went back to Dr. P. It was a pretty bad ride to his office. Everybody was mad. Even Austin. I don't get what THAT was about. It's not HIS stupid life!

So Dr. P. calls me in, and we're playing Foosball and we're talking. He's all, "I guess you're not feeling too good about things right now," and I'm, "Yeah. You could say that."

So we start talking, and I don't know what it is about that guy, but he's just…easy to talk to, you know? Turns out that we were doing the "What's the Rule?" thing all wrong. That's why it didn't work.

We talk and he tells me the secret to doing homework. It's called the Six G's.

1. Get it (from teachers)
2. Get it into (backpack)
3. Get it home
4. Get it done
5. Get it packed (backpack)
6. Get it back (to teachers)

So, here's **What's the Rule?** for me.

1. I write in my Planner for every subject. I don't leave class without writing the homework assignment down in it. If I have no homework, I write NONE.

2. I check my backpack before I go to practice to see that I have all my right books and folders.

3. I make sure I HAVE my backpack after practice.

4. Homework is from 7:30 – 8:30 at the kitchen table; I get to ask for help 3 times, no more. I ONLY do homework. If I get done early, I can read a book at the table.

5. When I'm done, I pack it up. THEN I get to watch TV and chillax!

6. The backpack is already packed and by the back door, so I just have to pick it up and go.

MMMMMM! yummy!!!

After Dr. P. we went out for pizza. They give you these Cinnamon Rolls that are SWEET!

So, before Christmas vacation, I was in American History 1 before class talking to Astrid, who was drawing her little…creatures…all over her notebook. Mrs. W. asks me if I'm going to enter the Science Fair. I tell her that I want to do something on Global Warming, but that probably everyone else was doing it. She asks Astrid, who says if she was going to enter, that would be what she'd want to do it on, but that she probably wouldn't…enter. Mrs. W. goes, "Why not?" and Astrid says about not being a techie or even understanding most of the projects and if everyone else is doing it…Global Warming…why bother?

So Mrs. W. goes, "Well, it seems to me

that you two have shared interests and complementary talents."

I'm sure we both looked completely blank, because Mrs. W. goes, "You, Astrid, can draw anything — and make it funny." I think she was looking at a cartoon of the Superintendent, sitting at his desk, lips all puckered up like he was going to kiss it, and wearing a big Dunce cap — in case you might miss it, the hat said **D–U–N–C–E** on it.

"And you, Maxwell, are very knowledgeable about technology. I saw the video you put together for Mr. Rollins on the Depletion of the Rain Forest. Most impressive."

I was stunned. Mrs. W. was giving me a compliment. Me — the guy who called her Mrs. Wart.

"The two of you might want to consider joining forces, and doing a project together — perhaps an animated film about Global Warming. With Astrid's characters and your expertise, I think you'd have a winner."

Then, Mrs. W. goes, "Isn't Austin taking that AP class at the college in video? I'm sure he could help you get some equipment to use."

I go, "But I wouldn't want to have anybody else do my project — in spite of what Grumpy Gus said in that memo." Boogerheaded me! I could have crawled through the floor!

But Mrs. W. just gets a little smile and goes, "Grumpy Gus. That's a new one." And then she mumbles something about "that memo" and laughs.

So Matilda goes, "So? Are you and Astrid going to do it?"

I told her I hadn't really thought about it.

So Matilda goes, in her strange Matilda way, "SO what are you waiting for? I think it's a terrific idea, Mrs. Ward has already given her imprimatur (I had to look it up; it means a seal of approval), and neither

Seal Of Approval

you nor Astrid has another partner. You and Astrid and me and Jake — I bet you guys could win. Seriously. Call Astrid — NOW!"

So, I did.

AND WE WON!

We took Best of Fair. The top prize.

Astrid was real happy. And I was pretty happy, too.

And my parents? Get a life, you guys! It was like I had done the greatest thing in the history of the world. Lame. But pretty cool.

And my teachers said they were proud of me.

Even Austin was all over it. And, he was pretty helpful. He's still a butthead. No, he's okay. It's hard for him to show me how to do stuff, when he could just DO IT faster and easier. But, that's not the point — as Dr. P. said. The point is to "help Maxwell develop the skills he needs to succeed in school and in life." I guess.

So, **What's the Rule?** is still on — and it's a good thing. I'm back doing homework in the kitchen. I do my homework after dinner, my Mom sits and goes through her recipe files and doesn't cook …and it doesn't bother me when she does, because she shuts her phone off. After Dr. P., she said, "My clients can live without me for one hour."

It's kind of nice. She's sitting, reading, or she's cooking, and it usually smells good, and it doesn't feel like prison, you know what I mean?

My Dad helped me to get my backpack organized, and he took me to the office store to get color-coded binders and file folders. He had me pick everything myself — which is nice because I know what works for ME.

Matilda looks at them and goes, "Nice. Color-coordinated and tasteful." Whatever.

I'm like, "I'm glad you approve, Matilda." She's such a beanbrain!

So, **What's the Rule?** is basically that homework is from 7:30 to 8:30. If I need help, which I did or thought I did for a while, but now I really don't except a few times with math, I can ask for it up to three times. Anything more than that, As Dr. P says, is still "doing it for me." At first, I was...What's the deal?... because nobody would "do it for me," but that was kind of first grade. So, now I just do it.

The organization thing and actually staying in the moment, as my Mother says, are hard for me. It's better, though. I really am trying, and my teachers are pretty cool with it. Like, if I can do enough of the assignment to show I get it, that's okay. Of course, for some stuff...like LA...you have to do the whole essay or report or whatever.

Matilda has been good. She came up with this system where she calls me or I call her right when we get home. We check to make sure we both know what homework we have. So, if I forget something, she reminds me. She also suggested that I just bring all my books home every night, so I don't get stuck. I got a new backpack...I have a lot of books.

Now, I feel pretty confident, so I don't always bring my LA book home — it weighs like 200 LBS! I just do my LA reading and writing in Study Period, which I never used for homework before. Weird. You can actually STUDY during Study Period. It saves a lot of time.

Those books are seriously heavy!

HMMMPH!

But my grades are good. I'm back up to B's, and I have 2 A's:

• Science, no surprise there.

• American History 1 — surprise there. I like that class. Not in the nerdy, kiss-kiss way, like Franklin: "Oh, Mrs. Ward, that's so INTERESTING!" but in the real liking way. Franklin is such a booger-brain.

• I'm back to a B in gym. Like it really matters...but why don't I have an A?

AND I haven't missed Star Wars in weeks!

Call Matilda; forgot my Art essay topic list.

Found it. In my gym shorts? **Strange.**

Astrid is cool. I feel bad about third grade. She's not a disaster. Kids can be so mean.

CHAPTER FIFTEEN:

Valentine's Day! LOVE Is in the Air!

Pul-eeze!

Matilda's
Journal

Matilda

OMG! OMG! OMG! OMG! OMG! OMG!
THIS IS THE BEST VALENTINE'S DAY EVER!!!
OMG! OMG! OMG! OMG! OMG! OMG!

This is so amazingly, spectacularly, phenomenally (rare, unique, extra special) awesome, that I almost can't find the words to describe what happened today!

SPECTACULAR

OMG! OMG! OMG! OMG! OMG! OMG! OMG! OMG!

First of all, well, not first, exactly, but working backwards, as it were (ooh! I love that "as it were" thing; it was on **Glitter Girls** last night. I really do get so much valuable information from that show. I can't believe that my parents say it's stupid. L-A-M-E!!! Astrid's parents say it's stupid, too. They're stupid, poopid!

Anywho, since Astrid and Maxwell won the Science Fair (all because of ME of course. He NEVER would have asked her if I hadn't yelled at him!) they've been hanging out — like, a lot. Which is an excellent thing.

Because Maxwell and Jake are **BEST** friends, and Astrid and I are **BEST** friends, and Maxwell and I are **BEST** friends, and…so on. Therefore, the four of us are, like, always together, which is majorly cool! I'm, like, flying out of bed every morning to get ready for school.

So we are at lunch today, and Jake and I and Astrid and Maxwell are talking about something really important — I can't remember what, at the moment, but it was significant (major, important, Large) and Franklin comes over and tries to sit RIGHT between Jake and ME!

Where was I? Oh, right,

Matilda's Journal

anywho, Franklin the **boogerhead** says, "You guys are so gross! Kissy kissy! EEEUW!!!"

Then Jake says…OMG. I wish you could have been there!!! Jake says…wait for it…"Well, that's YOUR opinion."

And he says it so, you know, casually. Like, "please pass the peas" (except, of course, that I HATE peas and I would **never** ask anyone to pass them. They are gluey and just so nasty!).

He says it really coolly. And Franklin, who always has an answer, was *speechless*!!! SERIOUSLY!

Then…I could almost faint (I never have, actually, fainted, but I've wanted to. It seems like it would be so cool!)…

Jake actually touched my hand!!

And smiled at me!!!

It was absolutely the best Valentine's Day present ever!!!

When we got to American History 1, Mrs. Ward said, "Ladies and gentlemen, we shall be checking your Homework Journals today."

I, of course, had mine all filled out; I actually had to get a second one, because I had filled up the first one.

Well, it was seriously comical! First **WWIT** goes all pale, and says, "Ooh! Mrs. Ward! I feel so sick! May I PLEASE go to the Nurse??"

And Mrs. Ward (OMG! I love her!) says, "Certainly, my dear. You do look pale. **Just leave your Journal on my desk** before you leave."

HA!

Franklin is looking rather sick, too.

Since he's such a suck-up, I'd've thought he'd've had it all done. Not so much! I see Jake whispering to him, then he raises his hand...Franklin, not Jake.

"Mrs. Ward, um, I've fallen a little behind in my journaling."

"How far behind?" asks the wonderful Mrs. Ward.

"Um, like, a few weeks?"

So she says, "Show me what you have, Franklin, and I'll give you some extra points for honesty."

So Franklin gets his trademark snarky grin, and the wondrous Ward says, "However, I shall have to check it **every Friday from now on**."

Sweet!!!

But then I thought, "OMG! What about Maxwell???? He hasn't done, like, ANY Journal entries in...forever!"

I am totally stressing over this.

I was in absolute agony. I mean, Maxwell's

FINALLY getting his act together, you know? The kid is getting good grades. He's got a girlfriend. He won the top prize in the All-State Science Fair — and they did it all themselves, Gus You Total LOSER!

Maxwell has been my friend...forever, like, since nursery school. And — don't get me wrong — he's great! He's smart and funny and VERY loyal. But — he's not exactly the most... focused person. I mean...sit down and write 90-something Journal entries?????
Pul-eeze!!!!! Not in this life!! (I just realized...I absolutely adore exclamation marks!!! They make any sentence happy!!!)

I absolutely ADORE exclamation marks!

So, Ward the Wonderful gets to Maxwell. He gives her this little smile, and she takes his Journal. There's a paper sticking out, so she reads the paper. Then she gives him a little smile and a nod, and leafs through his Journal. She hands it back, and says, "Nice job, Maxwell."

So, I am Perishing (dying, expiring, passing away) with curiosity. ~~Anywho~~ Enough of that! ANYWAY, I sort of accidently tackled him on his way to the lockers and shoved him into the boys' gym.

"Matilda, you're gonna make me late," he says.

"Okay, Maxwell, tell me what you did."

"Okay. You got me! I robbed the llamas. I stashed all their bananas in the boys' locker room!" he snickers.

"Oh, ma-a-an! More stupid llama jokes," I say. "How did you do it???"

"Well, I waited until they were all asleep, then I snuck in, and hotwired their banana wagon," he says.

So I say, "Enough with the lame llama jokes!!! How did you get your Journal past Mrs. Ward? She's no dummy, and I know you didn't make up 80 or 90 entries. Let me see!" I demand, knowing that now, I have him. He may have fooled Mrs. Ward — I can't imagine how — but he'll never get it past me. HAHAHA!!! I stick my hand out...right in his face.

"Okay, Matilda. Chill! Here it is." And he hands me his Journal.

Matilda's Journal

There, in amazing abundance (plenty, wealth, large amount) was his Journal. There weren't 109 entries, but there were a lot... some were pretty long, too.

I was stunned!!!

"Maxwell," I stammered. I stuttered. "I'm sorry...it's just, ummm...I'm so..."

"Shocked? Stunned? Freaked out???" Maxwell replied.

"Well, yes...sort of." I felt suddenly like maybe I didn't know my best friend as well as I thought. I mean, gosh! This is Maxwell we're talking about! How did...when did...did the planet spin out of orbit and no one told me?????

The world

OMG!

Matilda's World

"Relax, Matilda," he grinned. "I kind of surprised myself. But you'd better shut your mouth, or the flies'll start to land in it."

And then, he sort of…
hugged me!!!!! (In a totally
brother way…not boyfriend.
NEVER!)

OMG!!! Maxwell just kind
of hugged me. I am living in
an alternate universe…but
it's sort of nice here…I think
I'll stay.

So then I hear a scream, and Franklin
goes running past us…with absolutely nothing
on but a towel and sneakers!!!!! OMG!
SHM…Pul-eeze!!!!!

CHAPTER SIXTEEN:

Honesty Is Seriously the Best Policy!

Maxwell's Journal

Maxwell

February 14

Here's what I hate about Valentine's Day:

• It is totally lame

• You're supposed to get stupid cards for your Mother

• It is totally lame

• Some boneheaded moron thought it up to make people buy junk for girls

• It is totally lame

• Girls get all gooney and stupid and wait for you to give them a mushy card or something

• It is totally lame

Here's what I like about Valentine's Day:

• It is totally lame

• Astrid bought me a Valentine's card — with a llama joke!

• It is totally lame, but in a nice — not totally stupid — way

Middle school is not all bad. It was a kind of rough year to begin with, but everything has gotten a lot better.

I actually like school. Don't spread it around; a guy has a certain image, and "liking school" isn't exactly the first thing you want people to think about you.

But everything is cool. Dr. P. came through. **What's the Rule?** sort of saved my butt. Mrs. Ward is the best. My friends are kind of dumb…but in the good way.

Today, Dr. German (the Big G) slipped on a banana peel in the Cafetorium…I kid you not…and skated right into Lunchroom Lucy. I thought I might die laughing. I said something to Matilda about how mad hilarious it was, and she goes, "What?" The girl is a space shot around Jake.

But the biggest surprise came from my brother Austin. He comes in Sunday afternoon, and says, "Guess who I bumped into today?"

So I go, "I should care?"

And he goes, "I think so."

So I go, "You obviously want to tell me, Austin, so knock yourself out."

And he goes, "Sarah Shapely. She's the sister-in-law of your Coordinator of Student Affairs, Colleen."

I'm beginning to get a scary little feeling of where this might be headed, but I don't want to look too eager...or worried...so I go, "Oh, yeah?"

And he goes, "Yeah. She said that her sister-in-law is doing an INVENTORY of the **HOMEWORK JOURNALS.**"

Now I'm starting to sweat like a llama.

But, I stay cool. On the outside. I go, "Oh, yeah? When?"

"Tomorrow," he says.

And then, I remember.

After we started **What's the Rule?** I actually did most of the writing. Okay, maybe not every single day. But every day I had homework.

Dr. P. said to do something in my Homework Journal first, then do Science. That way I don't have to worry about getting checked.

I tried. I hope it's enough.

So, I write Mrs. Ward a note. I tell her about when I started writing. I tell her the Journal is missing the part until I started **What's the Rule?** but that I did it afterwards.

I figure, she'll either understand...or not. But I think she will.

She did. Thank you, Mrs. Ward.

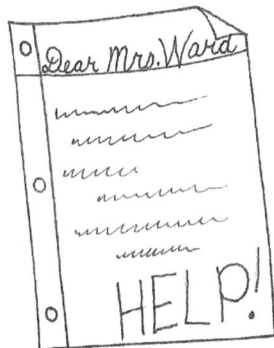

Dear Mrs. Ward

HELP!

So, Matilda was going nuts all during class. Most of it was really worry that I might get my butt kicked…but some of it was sheer morbid curiosity.

Then…after…she was all determined to catch me up. HA. She was really surprised when she saw my Journal.

Then she looked so…un—Matilda like. Sort of…humble. It made me feel kind of bad. So I gave her a hug. It was hilarious! For once, Matilda was speechless.

And then, Franklin! What a boogerhead!

A towel and sneakers?

But, seriously…it **was** the boys' gym!

THE END

Matilda's Naughty Word List

Education retention—it just sounds nasty

Urinal—only a boy could use something with such a yucky name!

Rectum—pul-eeze

Rectify—Sorry! It may mean "to correct" but it's just WRONG!

Slobber—the reason I like cats—they don't do this!

Spleen—who would even want one of these?

Vomitorium—even if Jake does say it, it's still disgusting

Rub-the-wrong-way—do I really need a reason?

Carpenter-Fincke—no explanation necessary!

We are ALL OVER the Web!

We – Matilda & Maxwell – have our own Facebook page! Come see us and write to us – we'll write back!

You can visit us there, or you can go to www.GoodParentGoodChild.com and find out all kids of cool stuff!

See you soon –
Matilda & Maxwell will be back!

www.ingramcontent.com/pod-product-compliance
Lightning Source LLC
Chambersburg PA
CBHW060506030426
42337CB00015B/1764